JESUS AND THE LITTLE CHILDREN

Bible Bedtime Story

BLUME POTTER

INTRODUCTION

In the hustle and bustle of today's world, finding the perfect bedtime story for your little ones is more important than ever. Jesus and the Little Children is more than just a collection of stories; it's a gateway to the love, kindness, and faith that Jesus showed to the children who gathered around Him.

This book offers a comforting, heartwarming way to introduce your children or grandchildren to the timeless lessons of the Bible. Through simple yet profound stories, it captures the special relationship Jesus had with children, teaching them that they are deeply valued and loved by God. Each story is crafted with care, making the lessons of faith, humility, and love accessible to young hearts and minds.

Reading these stories at bedtime will not only help your little ones drift off to sleep with a sense of peace and security, but it will also plant seeds of faith that will grow with them throughout their lives. These stories are perfect for quiet, cuddly moments, where the world slows down and your child or grandchild feels the warmth of God's love through the pages of this book.

Jesus and the Little Children is a treasure for every family, a must-have addition to your bedtime routine that will inspire, comfort, and teach the most important truths to the ones you love most.

CHAPTER ONE:
JESUS WELCOMES THE CHILDREN

Jesus walked through the towns and villages, His heart full of love and His words full of wisdom. Everywhere He went, people gathered to listen to Him talk about God's love. His stories were simple yet powerful, filled with hope and kindness, and everyone, young and old, felt drawn to Him.

One day, as Jesus sat under a shady tree, speaking to a crowd, a group of parents approached. They held the hands of their little ones, leading them toward Jesus with eager hearts. The children were excited, some holding small flowers they had picked along the way, hoping to give them to the kind man they had heard so much about.

But as they neared, the disciples stepped forward. They thought Jesus was too busy teaching important things to be bothered by children. "Please, take the children away," they said gently to the parents. "Jesus has much to do today."

The parents hesitated, feeling unsure. The children, too, looked up with wide eyes, their smiles fading as they saw the disciples turning them away. But before anyone could leave, Jesus noticed what was happening.

"Wait," Jesus said, His voice calm and full of warmth. He stood up and walked toward the children, His eyes filled with kindness. "Let the children come to Me," He continued, smiling at the little ones. "Do not stop them, for the kingdom of heaven belongs to such as these."

The disciples stepped aside, realizing their mistake, as Jesus knelt down to greet the children. The children ran to Him, their faces lighting up with joy. Jesus welcomed them with open arms, speaking to them softly and blessing each one. He took the time to listen to their tiny voices, to admire their flowers, and to show them that they were loved.

As the children gathered around Jesus, the crowd watched in awe. Jesus wasn't too busy for the children. In fact, He made it clear that they were just as important as anyone else. His love and attention were for everyone, especially the little ones, who He said had hearts pure and ready to receive God's love.

And so, that day, the children left with their hearts full of joy, knowing that they were precious in Jesus' eyes. The parents were filled with gratitude, understanding that their children had received a special blessing from Jesus Himself.

Jesus continued His journey, but the memory of those children stayed with Him, and His words remained in the hearts of all who heard them: "Let the children come to Me, for they are the heart of the kingdom of heaven."

CHAPTER TWO:
THE KINGDOM OF HEAVEN BELONGS TO THEM

As the children gathered around Jesus, He smiled at them warmly. Their eyes sparkled with curiosity and joy, and they listened intently, sensing that what He was about to say was important. The crowd, too, leaned in closer, eager to hear His words.

Jesus looked at the children, then at the crowd, and began to speak. "Truly, I tell you," He said gently, "unless you change and become like little children, you will never enter the kingdom of heaven."

The people were surprised by His words. They wondered what it meant to be like a child. Jesus continued, "The kingdom of heaven belongs to those who have hearts like these children—full of trust, innocence, and love. God loves the pure hearts of children and wants all of you to have that same simple, trusting faith."

The children beamed with pride, feeling special and loved. They understood that Jesus saw something wonderful in them, something that grown-ups could learn from. Jesus wasn't just talking about heaven; He was talking about how to live every day—with kindness, trust, and love, just like a child.

As Jesus spoke, the crowd began to understand. They realized that God didn't want them to be proud or boastful but to have hearts that were open and trusting, like those of children. The lesson was simple, yet it touched everyone deeply.

Jesus gently placed His hands on each child, blessing them and reminding them of their importance. The children knew they were precious in God's eyes, and the grown-ups saw the beauty of having a heart full of childlike faith.

With these words, Jesus showed that God's love is for everyone, but especially for those who approach Him with the pure, trusting hearts of children. And the children, filled with happiness, knew they were truly loved and cherished by Jesus.

CHAPTER THREE:
A LESSON IN HUMILITY

As the children sat close to Jesus, He looked at His disciples, who were still learning what it meant to follow Him. Sensing an important moment to teach them, Jesus began to tell a story.

"There were two men," Jesus said, "one was proud and thought he was better than everyone else. The other was humble, never thinking too highly of himself but always showing kindness and respect to others."

The disciples listened carefully as Jesus continued. "The proud man walked with his head held high, boasting about all he had done. He loved to be noticed and praised by others. But the humble man, though he had done many good things, never sought attention. Instead, he quietly helped others, always putting their needs before his own."

Jesus paused, allowing the lesson to sink in. Then He said, "In God's eyes, the humble man is greater than the proud man. Those who make themselves small, who do not seek to be noticed, are the ones who are truly great. Just like these children, who do not boast but come with open hearts, trusting and full of love."

The disciples nodded, understanding the importance of humility. They realized that they should not look down on anyone, thinking themselves better, but instead, welcome everyone with love, just as Jesus welcomed the children.

Jesus smiled at the children, who were still gathered around Him. "Remember," He said, "the greatest in God's kingdom are those who are humble, like these little ones."

The disciples knew then that following Jesus meant not just learning from Him, but also treating others with the same humility and love that He showed to all. They felt a new sense of purpose, determined to live out this lesson in their own lives.

And the children, feeling loved and valued, knew that in God's eyes, they were truly special, not because of anything they had done, but because of their pure and humble hearts.

CHAPTER FOUR:
JESUS HEALS THE SICK CHILD

One day, as Jesus continued teaching and healing the people, a father approached Him with a look of deep concern on his face. In his arms, he carried his young child, who was very sick. The father's eyes were filled with worry, but also with hope, for he had heard of the miracles Jesus had performed.

"Master," the father said, his voice trembling, "please help my child. He is very ill, and no one else can help him. I believe that You can heal him."

Jesus looked at the child with great compassion. The little one lay weak and pale, but Jesus saw beyond the illness to the heart of the child and the deep love the father had for his son.

Without hesitation, Jesus reached out and gently touched the child. He closed His eyes and prayed, asking God to heal the boy. The crowd watched in silence, their hearts filled with hope.

In an instant, the child's color returned, and he opened his eyes, looking up at his father with a bright smile. The sickness was gone, and the boy was full of life and energy once more. The father's eyes filled with tears of joy, and he hugged his son tightly, thanking Jesus over and over.

The people around them were amazed at what they had just witnessed. They marveled at Jesus' power to heal and at His deep love for the children.

Jesus smiled at the father and his child, then turned to the crowd. "Remember," He said, "God cares deeply for children. He listens to their prayers and the prayers of those who love them. Never doubt His love for the little ones."

The family left, their hearts overflowing with gratitude, knowing that they had experienced a miracle. And the people who had witnessed the healing knew that Jesus was truly special, filled with God's love and power, especially for the children.

Through this miracle, everyone understood that no matter how small or weak they might feel, God's love and care are always with them, and He is always ready to listen to their prayers.

CHAPTER FIVE:
A CHILD'S FAITH

As Jesus sat among the children, He began to tell them a story that would touch their hearts and teach them about the power of faith.

"There was once a young boy," Jesus began, "who had great faith in God. He loved to pray, and every time he did, he spoke to God with a pure and sincere heart. The boy believed with all his might that God would hear his prayers and answer them."

The children listened closely, their eyes wide with interest. The crowd around them grew quiet, eager to hear the lesson Jesus was about to share.

"One day," Jesus continued, "the boy's family was in need of food. They had very little to eat, and the boy could see the worry in his parents' eyes. But instead of feeling afraid, the boy knelt down and prayed to God. He asked God to provide for his family, trusting completely that God would help them."

The children leaned in, hanging on Jesus' every word.

"That very day," Jesus said with a smile, "a kind neighbor knocked on their door with baskets full of food. The neighbor had felt in his heart that he should share what he had with the boy's family. The boy's prayer had been answered, and his family had plenty to eat."

The children's faces lit up with joy at the story's happy ending. They understood that the boy's faith in God had been strong and true, and that God had listened to his prayer.

Jesus looked around at the children and the crowd. "A child's faith is powerful," He said softly. "It is pure, sincere, and full of trust. This is the kind of faith that pleases God. I want all of you to have faith like this young boy, believing with your whole heart that God hears you and cares for you."

With these words, Jesus blessed the children, placing His hands gently on each one's head. "You are all precious in God's eyes," He told them, "and He loves you deeply."

The children beamed with happiness, feeling special and loved. The grown-ups, too, were moved by Jesus' words, understanding that faith like a child's was something they should all strive to have.

And so, the story of the young boy with great faith stayed with them, reminding everyone that no matter how small they might be, their faith in God could move mountains. Jesus' blessing filled their hearts with peace, and they knew that they were truly cherished by God.